Library, Library

by Jay Sonoda • illustrated by Ken Laidlaw

Harcourt

Orlando   Boston   Dallas   Chicago   San Diego

Visit *The Learning Site!*
www.harcourtschool.com

Going to the Library

The library has many sources of information. Maybe you want to read a good story. Maybe you want to read your favorite magazine. You can find these sources in the library. Maybe you just want to find information on a topic. The library is the place for you!

The library has many different books. There are reference books, nonfiction books, and fiction books.

Reference Books

Imagine that you are writing a report. You have a topic. Now you will need to find information about the topic. You will use a reference book to find the information you need. A reference book provides information or help.

The first thing to do is to make a plan. What is your topic? Reference books contain information on topics such as music, art, science, history, computers, pets, and hobbies. What information do you need? Do you need to know where a country is, or information about its customs? Will you find the information in a dictionary, an encyclopedia, a thesaurus, an atlas, or another reference book?

You can find the reference book you need several different ways. You can ask a librarian for help. You can use a card catalog. You can use the library computer.

As you search for the book you need, make sure you have paper and a pencil or pen. You will need to write down information the librarian gives you or that you will get from the card catalog or computer.

The card catalog and the computer will tell you what kind of reference book you need and where to find it. Each type of reference book contains different kinds of information.

Reference books are usually kept in the same area. The dictionaries will be together. The encyclopedias will be together. The atlases will be together. The thesauruses will be together. Reference books cannot be checked out and taken home. You must use these books in the library.

Encyclopedia

An encyclopedia is a book or set of books containing information on many topics. A set of encyclopedias has a volume for each letter of the alphabet. A volume is part of a larger group of books.

The information in an encyclopedia is arranged alphabetically. Some encyclopedias contain information on one specific subject, such as art.

Suppose that you want to use an encyclopedia to find information on the subject of elephants. Which volume of the encyclopedia would you use to find this information? You would look in the volume *E* to find information on elephants.

You should use an encyclopedia to find general information about a topic. An encyclopedia will usually show a photograph or illustration of the topic. An encyclopedia also tells you where to find information related to your topic in other volumes.

Dictionary

A dictionary is a reference book that lists the words of a language in alphabetical order. A dictionary gives the meanings of these words. A dictionary will tell you if a word is a noun, an adjective, a verb, or another part of speech. A dictionary also gives information about how to pronounce words.

There are dictionaries that translate the words of one language into words of another language. There are also special dictionaries for certain topics, such as science.

Atlas

An atlas is a reference book that contains maps. An atlas shows the names and locations of different places. An atlas shows continents and oceans. An atlas shows countries and states. An atlas shows mountains, plains, and other land forms. An atlas also shows lakes, rivers, and other bodies of water.

An atlas may show cities and roads. Many atlases have information about a country or city's climate and population.

Thesaurus

A thesaurus is a reference book that is similar to a dictionary. A thesaurus lists words in alphabetical order. It also lists synonyms and antonyms for words. A synonym is a word that means the same, or almost the same as another word. An antonym is a word that means the opposite of another word.

You can use a thesaurus to find a word to replace another word. Suppose you are writing a report. You want to find another word for *nice*.

If you look up the word *nice* in a thesaurus you would see a list of other words that mean the same thing. You might see words such as *good, likable, pleasant,* or *sweet.* Many writers use a thesaurus to make their writing more exciting. Writers do not want to use the same words over and over. They want to use many different words to keep their readers interested. Maybe a writer wants to replace a word that he or she has used before. He or she can look in a thesaurus for a new word.

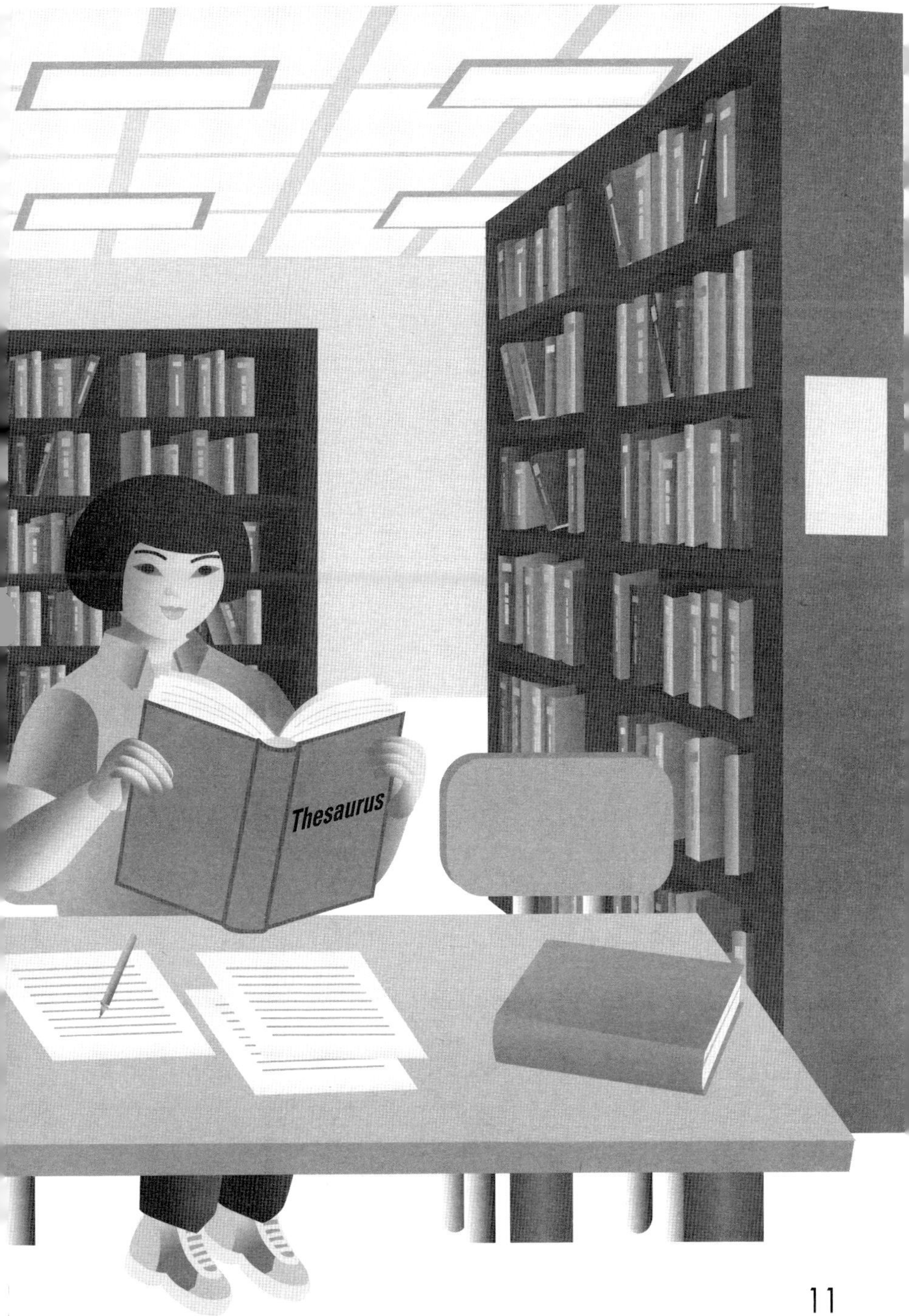
Thesaurus

Nonfiction Books

Nonfiction books are about facts and real events. The nonfiction books in a library are put on the shelves in number order. If you know the number of a book, you can find it quickly.

Here's another way the numbers can help you. All the books about a subject have the same or similar numbers. If you find one book about a topic, there will be others close by.

You may find lots of books with the same number. They are organized on the shelf by the author's last name.

12

Choosing a Nonfiction Book

How do you choose a nonfiction book? If you need specific information, you can look at the table of contents.

The table of contents tells what is in a book. It tells the titles of the book's chapters. It also tells the page numbers on which each chapter starts. You can look at the table of contents to see if the book has the information you need.

How to Train Your Dog

Table of Contents

Chapter 1: Sit .... page 3
Chapter 2: Come .... page 7
Chapter 3: Stay .... page 11
Chapter 4: Down .... page 15
Chapter 5: Good Dog! .... page 21

Fiction Books

Suppose you don't have to write a report. You just want to read a good story. To find stories about imaginary people, places, and things, look for the fiction books. These books are grouped together in a special place in the library.

Fiction books are about imaginary people and events. The fiction books in a library are organized on the shelves by authors' last names. If you know the author of the book, you can find the book quickly.

For example, if you want to read a book called *Henry Huggins* by Beverly Cleary, the book would be on the shelf with books by authors whose last names start with the letter C.

What if you don't know an author's last name? You can look for the title of the book on the computer or in the card catalog. Then you will find the author's last name. You can also search for fiction books by subject.

Fiction

Leaving the Library

When you find a nonfiction or fiction book you want to read, you can check it out. This means that you can take the book home. You need a library card to check out a book. The librarian can help you get a library card.

Usually you must bring the book back to the library in two or three weeks. This should be enough time to read the book. If you need more time, you can check it out again.

Now you know what the library has to offer. What books will you look for on your next trip to the library?